THE CARNIVORE

David R. Slavitt

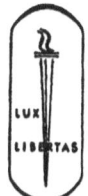

THE UNIVERSITY OF NORTH CAROLINA PRESS
CHAPEL HILL
1965

Contemporary Poetry Series
Copyright © 1963, 1964, 1965 by David R. Slavitt
Some of the poems in this volume have previously appeared in
The Kenyon Review, The New Republic, and *The Yale Review.*
Library of Congress Catalog Card Number 65-13668
Printed by the Seeman Printery, Durham, North Carolina
Manufactured in the United States of America

For Lynn

Who koude telle, but he hadde wedded be,
The joye, the ese, and the prosperitee
That is bitwixe an housbonde and his wyf?

CONTENTS

ITEM FROM NORWICH · *3*
THE LEMMINGS · *5*
THE ENIGMATIC DEATH OF THE EMPEROR, ALEXIUS—A.D. 1081 · *6*
PLANTING CROCUS · *7*
MOZART · *8*
FINANCIAL STATEMENT · *9*
RIDE THE HIGH COUNTRY · *10*
CHILD WITH DOG · *11*
IN DEFENSE OF ARCADIUS—A.D. 396 · *12*
MAQUILLAGE · *13*
ON REALPOLITIK AND THE DEATH OF GALBA · *14*
NURSERY RIME · *15*
DA VINCI SUNSET · *16*
F. A. O. SCHWARZ · *17*
CENTRAL PARK: APRIL · *18*
THE CARNIVORE · *19*
STAURACIUS · *20*
A SHORT TROT WITH UCCELLO'S HORSES · *21*
ON THE WASHINGTON WIRE · *22*
VARIATIONS ON AN ANCIENT THEME · *23*
MOUSE · *24*
STILL LIFE · *27*

THE SCHOOL OF ATHENS · *28*
EPITAPH FOR MY WIFE'S GREAT AUNT · *30*
DISCUSSION, BACK HOME · *31*
THE WRECKERS · *32*
COLLOQUY BETWEEN TWO KINGS · *33*
FAMILY HISTORY · *34*
A VICTORY FOR THE EASTERN EMPIRE · *35*
DISTRESSED FINISH · *36*
GRENADE FISHING · *37*
LOVE POEM · *38*
ST. PATRICK'S DAY: 47TH STREET · *39*
ELEGY · *40*
CESSNA 170 · *41*
TREE WORSHIP · *42*
THEODORIC · *43*
FIRST SNOW · *44*
BELISARIUS · *45*
SPECULATIONS ABOUT THE DEATH OF ESKIMOS · *46*
HALF FARE: A SUITE FOR EVAN · *48*
   London
   Barcelona
   Rome
   Florence
   St. Tropez
   Vezelay
   Paris
   The Channel
   Vienna
   Paris
   Venice
   Vevey
   Avignon
   Copenhagen
ELEGY FOR WALTER STONE · *55*

THE
CARNIVORE

ITEM FROM NORWICH

The bit before the baseball scores: the man
seventy-two, found in a tarpaper shack
somewhere around the city dump he scavenged,
dead for a week. And underneath his mattress,
bankbooks with ninety-seven thousand dollars
and some odd change. It always makes the news,
sure-fire, like goldfish swallowing, flagpole sitting,
and the other traditional mortifications.
                                                        The Syrian,
Simeon Stylites, raised near Antioch
a column three feet around and sixty high,
on top of which the heat of thirty summers,
the cold of thirty winters he weathered, praying
in all the different postures of devotion:
erect, with arms akimbo as the cross,
or bowing forehead to feet, which exercise
was observed—twelve hundred and forty-four repetitions
(at length the weary spectator gave up).
The patient Simeon died atop his column.

In the regimen of the Egyptian monasteries:
two small biscuits (Paximacia loaves),
six ounces each; boiled vegetables to be served
but never eaten; on feast days a little cheese
or a small fish of the Nile. At Oxyrinchus,
thirty thousand monks adored such a fish
in the "magnificent temple" of Strabo's mention.

                                        Novitiates
in our fraternities compare them to vitamin pills,
except when they flip their tails as they go down.
And the man by the dump—today's report is from Norwich—
followed the dictates of the Caesarian Basil;
the laws of Martin of Tours; of Hilarion,
who left disciples in Sicily and Epirus
as well as Cyprus; of the Coptic Antony.

The impulse is with us always. Gestures survive:
testing has ruined the sea turtles' sense of direction,
and after they come ashore to lay their eggs
they continue forward, crawling away from the water
to die of exhaustion in the inland grasses.
Their brains roasted by sun, in the final moments
their flippers resume that sweep in the dry sand
of swimming, of riding the currents of the lost sea.

THE LEMMINGS

Food short against the long days' hunger, sunset
a fatty morsel in the western broth, and sick
of racing the birds and the tides on the sandspit
for bits of edible sea wrack at which to pick,

it seems no more unreasonable one day
to try at last that sea which somewhere reaches
a western landfall where each footfall may
fester with food, where it rolls down the beaches.

Thus their Columbus argues, convincing them,
for who has the strength to discuss or even care?
Slowly, like a tide, they begin to swim
westward in the nobility of despair.

And if they never return, who can say the conclusion
is the obvious drowning it probably all comes to
who has stared for twenty minutes at the horizon
where the herring silver touches the herring blue?

THE ENIGMATIC DEATH OF THE EMPEROR, ALEXIUS—A.D. 1081

Skillful Alexius, brave Alexius, Turks,
dead, attested your greatness, and dead Normans.
The house of Comnenus you brought back at last
and the richness of Constantinople—the glitter, the grace,
the proper air of our pre-eminent city.

Then why do we hear, when you lay on your deathbed,
that one word of the Empress Irene,
the shriek, and the shriek's echo along the halls:
"Hypocrite," with hysterical female sobbing,
and read upon your tombstone, "Hypocrite"?

PLANTING CROCUS

I know the violet's faith, the columbine's
ingratitude, have read and remember so
(rosemary's that). Tangled like unpruned vines,
old lines of garden poems choke the garden;
the pollen of weeds from Twickenham, Eden, Arden,
settles on my plot. The man with the hoe
haunts me, that gruesome woman by Greuze taunts.

The crocus is impatience. The mesh sacks
of bulbs bear pictures of next season's blooms,
a chaste blue for the love of his Smilax.
And I know all about him, except how deep,
how far apart to plant, how he will keep,
how rise six months from now from these small tombs,
know nothing of how his onions grow.

I cultivate my garden. Even to say it
takes nerve, but the trowel helps and the smell of the bed
and the scratch of my digging on its rocks of quiet.
My son helps too, dropping bulbs in the holes
and tamping the ground smooth with his small soles.
He is certain the flowers will come, because I have said
they would. And will they? I can only pray.

I have not mentioned to him the old, dead
bulbs of last year. That owner's hope was high
and a few of his tulips came up, handsome blood-red,
but he had planted many more than we got.
I find the rest of them now, beginning to rot.
The impatience of Crocus is nothing at all to my
own to see all the blossoms or some or none.

MOZART

If Mozart whistled airs *in utero*
or passed the time while he was sucking his bottle
    fingering it as practice for the oboe,
you produced sprung rhythms with your rattle,
    babbled in twelve tones your ethereal
serial music, while eating your cereal.

    But it will not work, it will not. You have composed
    nothing, play nothing but the phonograph,
and you are five now—nearly five and a half—
who can carry only precariously a tune.
    In the afternoons, when Mr. Mozart dozed,
little Wolfgang used to play the buffoon—

    played the piano I mean: progressions of chords,
incompletely, and the old man had
to get up, bang the tonic, say gruff words
    and then go back to his nap. Pick out the line
    of "Jingle Bells," the commercial for Mr. Clean,
and I would bound from your mother's embrace to applaud.

    I had got used to my not being Mozart,
    but in a son's first year what father's heart
has never fluttered once, imagining,
    with little enough reason, despite more ...
I love you as myself. Badly I sing
a lullaby to your tin ear, heartsore.

FINANCIAL STATEMENT

Benjamin Franklin, egomaniac, lecher,
a penny saved is a penury earned. Your eye
upon this donut, brother: "Fresh Tuesday"
but bought on Wednesday. It is a meek new world,
the saving of six cents an exercise
of the soul. The hair of heroes, the hair of angels,
and angels' harps are all the color of money,
and heaven shines like a bank vault, but copper is hell
and the deepest pit is the penny black with holding,
coin of the common people, Lincoln's friends,
slaves still.
          The taste is nearly the same.
But when it came back from the waters, all ninefold,
it was not day-old 27¢
as are these donuts,
                    which were a deliberate choosing.
The finitude grows like a fungus. Destitute Dick,
does your almanack tell me where is fancy bread?

I think of my infant daughter's ravening
and know what Adam hoped against all knowledge:
that somehow his sons would escape to have their fill
of all the best that he had had until
that marked-down, day-old apple ended it.

RIDE THE HIGH COUNTRY

I
The long red underwear of Randolph Scott,
the gold-rimmed spectacles of Joel McCrea,
underscore age, and through the reverend plot
the old gunfighters ride for one more day.

And Ladd was old in *Shane,* and in *High Noon*
old Coop had all his wrinkles emphasized
(with visible distaste he drew his gun).
The ritual of honor is disguised

and is an act of memory and will.
The pistol packing, popcorn eating child
feels the pretended stubble on his chin
and imagines his bones weary after the kill.
Even the movies' west is no longer wild,
its *virtu* now a trail bum, a has-been.

II
Odysseus, safe at home, can be our friend.
Orestes and the Furies come to terms
—our terms: we, craven, crave the tamest end,
the fireside remembrances of storms,

the hero's diminution. The old hand
is slower on the draw, the eyes are gone.
We may admire, but we understand
that nerve is all McCrea is working on,

that aged manliness becomes absurd.
He makes mistakes out on the trail, he has
fallen into their obvious trap, is hit,
and crumples with gun blazing. On the hard
ground he shakes our comfort as he dies,
affirming the agelessness of what is fit.

CHILD WITH DOG

She hesitates to uncross her legs, to shift
the position of her arms; her breathing
is suddenly conscious, counted.

Beside her, on the couch, the dog
shows the red haws of sleep, the flanks of sleep.
At an automobile horn, the ear twitches,
is still again. Her nose itches,
and arms are lead,

but bathing in the attention of the sleeping animal,
rapt in the concentration of the dog,
focused upon her in the brindle sleep
she carefully preserves,
she is reluctant to disturb the dog,
reluctant to disturb the dog sleeping,
reluctant to disturb.

IN DEFENSE OF ARCADIUS—A.D. 396

Outside they carried Rufinus' head on a pole
and crowds cheered, while in the taverns soldiers
played with the severed hand, opened the fingers,
and said, "Give to the insatiable."
They got free drinks. But now Eutropius
stands in the same place, at the emperor's ear,
and is no better than Rufinus was.

The emperor is nevertheless beloved.
They say he is feeble-minded. So, he drools.
But no one can say Arcadius is dishonest.

MAQUILLAGE

A tremor of the lash; the porcelain silence
glazes the bathroom tiles and silvers the face
that follows the other in the silvered glass,
and the hand which in most delicate assurance
twitches the gold of the mascara case,
stopping the breathing of both those low-backed bras.

Dumb on the rim of the tub, I watch you stare
your image down, and then appraise it as
a man might try a weapon, slashing air.
That momentary, cerebrated gaze
dissolves reflection, flesh, to leave bare bone
of beauty's calculation. In the cold
of white tile wall, white basin, tub, and bowl
I wait, and you return, and turn. "All done."

ON REALPOLITIK AND THE DEATH OF GALBA

The Emperor Galba was bald as a bowling ball,
and thus the soldier carried the hacked head,
a thumb in the mouth of the ruler of seven months,
to Otho of ninety-five days.
                        There are some that say
the death of Galba was noble, some say not.
He was the first outside of the Julian line
to wear the imperial purple. He was the first
to assume the purple elsewhere than in Rome.
Some blame him for the one thing, some the other,
or both, or neither.
                    But everyone agrees
Galba was stingy. Who then can criticize
the perhaps inelegant style of the soldier's strike?

NURSERY RIME
For Joshua

bo
peep
little bo peep
little old bittle old o bo peep

old bo peep
little bo peep
little ittle bo pittle ittle o peep
o o peep
little old peep
bittle ittle odle ittle o bittle peep bo
odle ittle peep bo
little bo peep

hey diddle diddle and a little bo peep
little bo diddle hey little bo peep
fiddle faddle peep hey
bo bo peep hey
little diddle he pay
heap peep peep

bo
peep
little bo peep
had a little ho ho
good bye peep

DA VINCI SUNSET

Michelangelo's paint pots and Raphael's cartoons
weary the master. Tired of pictures, he spends his afternoons
discussing mirrors with the Germans,
arguing optics and light,
or experimenting with varnishes to get the formula right.
    Leonardo has become
    intrigued by a grander medium.

For the Holy Father's datary, he has done a Madonna and Child.
The picture, he said, was nothing, but the pigments, he said, were
    wild.
And now he is making a lizard
into a dragon with wings.
He has fashioned horns and a beard for it: his art form now is things.
    Leonardo has become
    intrigued by a grander medium.

The wings are constructed of lizard scales, by quicksilver attached
to the back of his lizard dragon. He has said to those who have
    watched:
"Buonarroti, flat on his back,
could lie for a thousand years,
but before those fingers move to meet, my dragon will wiggle his ears."
    Leonardo has become
    intrigued by a grander medium.

Now he is making animals of a wax of a certain kind
and by shaping them thin and hollow and filling them with **wind**
he makes them fly around the room.
He is crazy, people say.
He calls Pygmalion fool and says all pictures are child's play.
    Leonardo has become
    intrigued by a grander medium.

F. A. O. SCHWARZ

> "... *would needsly scorse,*
> *A costly Jewell for a Hobby-Horse...*"
> —Michael Drayton

More than their children, they too are pretenders
whose tykes on trikes, their sons, they see sun-kings,
and bear them, like ambassadors, such baubles
as Fabergé designed and moneylenders
reckoned in years of taxes. And Schwarz's things
have still that high contempt of a million rubles.

Though crowns be gone, God save the attitude
of the dauphin playing with his cup and ball
as if to dare goddams to shake his throne.
On a four-hundred-dollar horse a diminutive dude
can look dispassionately on the fall
his France is threatened with, and wait for Joan.

"A Jewell for a Hobby-Horse"? The exchange
is better than fair. With the toy's extravagance
they mark the child as the last of royalty
who gallops, careless of their broadloom range,
and, sharing his noble disdain of circumstance
(his kingdom is a horse), swear loyalty.

CENTRAL PARK: APRIL

A season of tops and radios; the sun,
sponged by the fitful breeze at the tingling point
of perspiration, while loud children run
the park into the eyelid's blood-red streaming
(the shouts, the music, growing ever more faint),
sets the sprawled women, strolling young men dreaming.

This first voluptuary day in the park,
this Sunday soaking of light and warmth on benches,
and into prams and onto blankets where dark
glasses are put aside, skirts hiked up, wrenches
the year around in a suddenly glimpsed moment:
her, for example, running rather to fat,
asleep in the sun and showing a small extent
of winter-white thigh, sharp as the crack of a bat.

THE CARNIVORE

Inward beyond the bone, the grazing beast
glides like a fish in water among real fish
that swim the rippling sinews, silver still,
but know brown lowing too in fields of flesh.
Lion and lamb, the salmon and the steer
lie down together in my wheaten meadow,
wander within my orchard of apple and pear
and live serenely, past my pearly gates.
For heaven is all hunger: the high hawk
chews the chipmunk's terror out of him,
teaches him lessons of soaring, swooping—and learns
white oiliness of acorns. The oak's patience
first furred is feathered now and sees the green
blur of its whole hill in the carnivore.

I speak with the logic of wafers and sips of wine,
forbidden camels and swine, the sacred cattle,
and all the days of fasting and feast days:
the theological etiquette Isaac learned,
bound like an eye roast on the carving board
and, wet to drowning in God's spittle, spared.

And therefore am I vineyards, orange groves,
broad wheat fields and the depths of moving oceans
where I have raced in terror of my nets,
have preyed upon myself and died, eating
animal and herb with the dull love
the rat, the buzzard, and the worm bear me.

STAURACIUS

Stauracius was wounded, was slowly bleeding to death.
They named him emperor, nevertheless. He reigned
for six months, sicker every day
of the constant squabble about the succession. At last
he proposed neither Michael, his brother-in-law,
nor his own blood brother—but a democracy.

The city was outraged, and Michael had no choice
but to assume the purple, Stauracius
not yet having died, though now aware
that an emperor can be killed, can be shut up
in a monastery, can die. Even the worst
cannot evade such kindnesses at the end.
A majority is much more to be feared:
a many-headed monster, it lives forever.

A SHORT TROT WITH UCCELLO'S HORSES

Sir John de Hawkwood rides a sea-green horse
on a field plum-purple, up on the north wall
of this "somewhat bare and chilly" Duomo, echo
of the deeper green outside of the Prato marble
or simply a kind of cinquecento whimsy...
this pistachio prancing.
                        Friars ride their Vespas,
their rope ceintures whipping the wind, and women
in broughams to Ferragamo's nibble *gelati*:
for Sir John, why not a light lime-phosphate horse?
But in the Uffizzi, Uccello's sketch omits
any rider at all, and upstairs in Battaglia
(and in Paris, Bataille; in London, Battle) horses
of the same feather trample the true enough gore,
but smiling with carousel glee.
                             They are not monsters,
do not have heads of tigers, wings of birds,
or tails of vipers seven times coiled. Sir John,
on a green griffon, a yellow yale, could ride
whatever walls he would, and with surer seat
than on this horse that is not a horse, this beast
that is no beast.
                  Over a Strega with ice
that night in the Piazza della Signoria
you said, "The odd thing in the way the city looks
is its natural feeling of power. That homey fort,"
you said, and nodded toward the Palazzo. Horses
are also tame, and those old condottieri
rode them unthinking, as polo players can;
but a green horse that is no horse, those grinning
beasts in Uccello's canvases, whose riders
are irrelevant holders of spears, fountains of blood,
are deceptive as power, as wild, as giddy, as green.

ON THE WASHINGTON WIRE

*The Shah of Iran addresses
the Washington Press Club, June, 1962.*

Truth should be difficult: one
wishes a riddling rune,
allusions to the Wallachian,
puns in Walloon;
but in easy English, to the press,
the king of Persia
in correctly Western dress
declares, "This king business has
given me personally nothing but headaches."
The secret of the Shahs
is out, learned hard, by mistakes.
It is not news. From Darius down,
this world business has
given nobody personally anything but headaches,
in Baghdad, Teheran, Bergen Park,
or any fortified city, or unfortified town.

VARIATIONS ON AN ANCIENT THEME

Fellah farms while frigatoon
ferries fangots featly;
I fetch my feeze for the farandole
and the end of fending
at the nightfall.

Unbraced, unpinned, unbreeched, unbound,
the moon unblemished rises,
unsays ukase of urgent day,
restores Ursprache
usquebaugh's way.

Cumbent creatures rouse to cruise,
crave cock-a-hoop consortium:
caliph carousers, caitiff canoodlers,
they pair and creep
to their cozy croodlers.

Kakapo cries and kea gorges
on the kidney fat of sheep.
In a kajawah my love comes
across the karroo
and the kanoon thrums.

MOUSE

I

Death have I dealt six times;
have flung the trap with sprung
bar behind small skull
(the neck smartly snapped
as the dark gout at the ear
bore witness) down the incinerator;
have with my shoe heel crushed
the trapped skittering still;
have once with a mop handle
mauled a mouse to meat
and done with the mess in a dustpan.
Truce, for the time, with the roaches:
my war now is with mice,
the rattling noise in the broiler,
the droppings I find in the broom closet,
the grey blur, only distinct
in its tail, that darts by the dishwasher
to behind the stove. It is war.
With pleasure I bait the mousetrap,
with glee I trip the lever,
imagining into the thwack
the fragility of the neck,
and carefully on the linoleum
I lay the temptation down.
Six have I killed in a month now.
The last of them seems to be trap-shy.

II

A week and still he lives,
offends like a frayed cuff
or a gaping hole in the pocket
of the garment of my composure.
I should have thought such hatred
would have to be earned. I have watched
my dog stalking the mouse,

ears cocked and breathing shallow,
her anus tightened, freezing
at the familiar noises,
freely intent on her quarry
and the simple pleasure of killing.
Twice I have seen her lunge,
miss by a breath, and walk off
serene in her sense of the odds
who must beat out the mouse but once.
I am no sportsman about it:
I heard it last night in the oven
and turned on the gas—did not light it
but hoping for asphyxiation
left it to hiss at my victim,
until I could no longer bear it.

III

The mouse is dead—not I
but the cleaning woman killed it,
most casually on the counter,
crushing it there with the breadbox
behind which it ran for shelter.
I should have liked to have done it,
not for the satisfaction
of ridding the kitchen of vermin,
nor for any pride of the kill,
though it certainly took some deftness—
but it had become my mouse
living with my hatred.
Now it is no longer with us
and I almost regret its passing—
from which I can draw no moral
saving that cleaning women
should be in attendance always.
Like mice, their occasional presence
disturbs the whole fabric of living.
For my children, the custom of servants
I wish most sincerely, or none
and ease with the mice of the world

with immunity to the diseases
I have always supposed that they carry,
but immunity more to disgust
at swift-footed, naked-tailed rodents
and quick-legged, shiny-backed bugs.

STILL LIFE

Hanging like crystal from a salon ceiling,
their phrases glint among the curios,
carry that same slight, expensive feeling
of this fragile objet d'art, or that belle chose,
and settle on a Louis Quatorze chair.
And yet, for all the talking in the room,
there is Miranda, standing on the stair,
a figure out of some Egyptian tomb.

THE SCHOOL OF ATHENS

The barbarous Illyrian, Upranda,
styled himself Justinian. His Greek
was, nonetheless, laughable, fitting only
for adjudication of circus brawls, speeches
in the worst taste (I mean the dedication
of Anthemius' church, that ghastly flat-domed wonder),
and Constantinople U.
                            But this crude mouth
brought an end to the School of Athens, and severed
the golden chain that stretched to the time of Plato
who was no Christer either.
                          Then the professors
Diogenes, Eulalias, Hermias,
Priscian, Damascius, and Isidore
and master Simplicius, departed for Persia.

There, it was rumored, existed the Republic:
there was Chosroes, the philosopher king,
and every kind of virtue Socrates
had conjured up in Polemarchus' house.
The huge rubies, the tiger skins from Persia,
the spices, the fabled lushness of vegetation
hinted the excellence of that rare land,
where, with the men, the women were taught gymnastics,
Sicilian cookery was banned, and Corinthian orgies,
and all things were harmonious, and good.

In ships they went, making most perilous voyage,
and across rough country, and dusty and cold,
these elderly professors with their books,
and came at last to Persia.
                       But the soul
did not order the mind, or the mind the body
in Persia either, but lasciviousness
held sway of government and courtesans
were better loved than logic. Corinth was pure
and the food in Syracuse most plain and wholesome

compared to Persia. There, ignoble nobles,
discourteous courtiers and foolish wise men
amused the king who was philosopher
of vanity, ambition, cruelty...
And the dead were left exposed to the carrion birds.
And brothers married sisters as in Egypt.

They gathered their books again, and wept, and journeyed
back to the Empire's borders and civilization,
to live out their lives in tranquil misery,
agreement having been made in the treaty with Persia:
In consideration of eternal peace,
Justinian shall pay to Chosroes
eleven thousand pounds of gold, shall cede
the right to occupy Dara, shall guarantee
the lives and safety of these philosophers ((named))...
    Chosroes ((sigil)) et Upranda ((sigil))

Simplicius died last and with him Athens.

EPITAPH FOR MY WIFE'S GREAT AUNT

For sixty-eight years she turned her eyes
and her thoughts away from any unpleasant thing.
Her speech turned bankruptcy to the vaguer
"difficulty," vulgar divorce to "trouble."

When it forced its way into her conversation,
it came out her way, blandly—"passing on."
But what would she say now of her own death?

DISCUSSION, BACK HOME

On San Lorenzo's steps we sat down, tired
by then of interesting sacristies, thirsty, our feet
still feeling the Campanile from days before,
and said, "The hell with it, the hell with it all."
And you, old Cosimo, old George W. Medici,
Avrum ben Giovanni knew all about art
including its worth in lire—or time—and bargained
nicely, being lavish but no sucker;
you would have spent our forty minutes here
admiring your grave, and the idea
of going to Viareggio would have been yours.

"Cosi*mos*," he exclaimed, "with an 'S'! Cosi*mo* is the duke,
but the founder Cosi*mos*, pater patriae,
we always call Cosi*mos*. My God!" he said,
and gasped that we had left so lightly, wheeling
back to the buffet, and "Ah, Firenze!"
holding aloft the potato salad spoon.

*Different ideas of excellence, what men should do
and what they deserve*—insisting on that "S"
with his whole professor's heart. His trip, his life
we slighted on those steps. Your Fiesole hat
that you fanned yourself with, made the slightest possible breeze
and we thought of the breeze that the sea must be bringing in
and decided to stop for *gelati*, and then leave, leave
this city of precious tourismo. Cosimo
inside there knew history too: the blue tide
that sweeps the sand smooth each Riviera morning.

THE WRECKERS

They nibble, as at a cookie-house, from the gable,
chew chimneys, roof, snap off the second floor,
or scramble as small boys who for once are able
to wreak their havoc, wreck, hack, and wage war

on the old regime of respect for property.
They chuck, with those four-by-eights, all mothers' pro-
(and in-) hibitions out on the lawn on a spree.
But no crowds throng the street to watch it all go

as they come to watch steam shovels, the star actors
of the building trades' free sidewalk matinee
whose draw is the envy of all of the subcontractors.
Daily the house diminishes. As the grey

walls fall, they reveal the pink wallpaper
in indecent exposure. The naked sky
shows through the open ceiling. The rough raper
with his iron balls gives the porch the eye.

COLLOQUY BETWEEN TWO KINGS

Having met grief with honor, they are great—
even literally, for we sense their size
more than we hear their words at the city gate:
the stranger who has daughters for his eyes
offers protection to Athens out of his hate,
and Theseus listens and shows no surprise.

That two, whom the world has used so, should confront
one another, observe amenities, stand
on the same ground, would seem an outrageous stunt
some eager, tactless press agent had planned,
except that they only indirectly allude
to the signatures of intolerable grief:
the color of a sail, a fork in the road.
Their manners are what burden our belief.

FAMILY HISTORY

My father feared the Turks. My grandmother
had saved, like old buttons, fears of another
country, and worries a generation late
followed my father along all Bridgeport's dark
streets, with the threat that any moment great
swarms of scimitars from Seaside Park
would leave their trail of dying and of dead.
Nobody else in Connecticut shared his dread,
and he outgrew it, trading his private war
for the Bunker Hill and Malvern and San Juan
he studied in still-standing Bridgeport's classes—
which was the end of that conscript ancestor
the Tsar had sent to fight in Turkestan
and die on one of those nameless Caucasian passes.

A VICTORY FOR THE EASTERN EMPIRE

Eastward beyond the Oxus, Yezdegerd,
grandson of Chosroes and the last
Sassanian king of Persia, fled the sword,
Khalid, and the Moslems, seeking the aid
of Li Shih-min who was the T'ang T'ai Tsung,
acknowledged master of forty-four Tartar hordes,
to recover the leathern apron, the gold cuirass,
the fire that had burned twelve hundred years.

Beyond the Jaxartes, at Scythia, he proclaimed
his friendship with the T'ang, the interest of China,
and raised a Turkish army to retake Persia.
They turned against him, too. At a small stream,
he begged a miller with a little boat
to leave his milling for the afternoon
and row his king across. The haggling.
The offer of bracelets, refused. The demand for silver.
And Yezdegerd slew this miller. His son, Firuz,
shoved off in the boat, and the Turks came.
And Firuz, at the far bank, was an orphan.

He made his way along the Tarim River,
called there Hsi Yu, across the Shen Shen desert
and into Han and the capital, Ch'ang An.
And lived in Ch'ang An, as the King of Persia,
acknowledged thus by all, under T'ang T'ai Tsung,
and into the reign of Kao and the Empress Wu.

And Firuz named his son Ni-Ni-Shih.

DISTRESSED FINISH

Small drills emulate the work of worms,
insinuate into the wood the appearance of great
age. The expert workmen beat the arms
and worry the walnut legs to anticipate
those valued ravages that even good
care would show on ever more valued wood.
The fashion of course is decadent—the trunk
of the tree was hewn laboriously, worked
victoriously to Louis', to Plato's chair,
the immortal forms of a chair—but that belief
is long gone. The slow regression to junk
satisfies us who know, now, that ruin lurked
in the wood from the start, and who no more declare
the immortality of any form but grief.

GRENADE FISHING

A pull of the pin, a lob, a plunk in the lake:
and then that moment of rippled silence before
the grenade goes off, and the lovely dead fish break
the surface, themselves, in pieces. On the shore,
a lip-smacking of water. For hook and line
and the sickening tug of the fish like a frightened insect
skittering down there, give me the anodyne
grenade blast, honorable, direct.

Angels ascending, the fish float to the surface,
loll on their sides, single eye to heaven,
while fisher rows and scoops with illegal net.
The oars plash with clarity of purpose
in the lake, metal-smooth once more. Morning's at seven
and the fastest is the best death you can get.

LOVE POEM

Once when we touched, we both ached as if bruised;
we find more comfort now, which is worth keeping.
Long have we used each other's bodies, used
our bodies for each other, which then fell sleeping,

the spent flesh in its so familiar embrace—
and this is marriage. Still, at the foot of the bed,
disrobing, often I have found a trace
of shyness, an evasion of eyes, the head

inclined so—yours and mine—for the opening
of clothes, of closedness that covers over
the naked body, so familiar a thing,
but still a little strange, as when we were lovers.

ST. PATRICK'S DAY: 47TH STREET

Keep the girl who struts her stuff and twirls
that silver member, surrogate for those
others ranged behind her, keep her off this street.
Abandon Fifth to drumbeats, bagpipe skirls,
and marchers wearing the green. Green, I suppose,
is better than brown, though I've heard the German fleet

refueled sometimes at Ireland. I dislike
these terrors of my mother's childhood playground,
and the drums revive in me her forgotten fears
of the tough micks, as apt to flay a kike
as fly a kite. Massed bugles make a sound
like knives nicking these bearded Jews' old ears

who had, one day in Nuremberg, parades
enough to last them another five thousand years.
They stay indoors with their hoards of precious stones
while green pins, green ties, green fanfaronades
march and admire the marching. Occasional cheers
for the IRA, like moisture, make their bones

ache with rheumatic clairvoyance. Yes, I know
Yeats was a great poet, and the humor of Joyce
is very like Jewish humor. I remember a sign:
CATHOLICS STINK, and my amazement, though
not unmixed with relief that the mad voice
of mobs could cry for other blood than mine.

The Irish (if Australia's the mid-west
of the far-east) are surely the Jews of the north.
But to see them marching in this street is dumb
grief, is the woe of warring at my breast,
is the orange rage I feel, blossoming forth
at the ghettos and post offices in that drum.

ELEGY

A homely grief, grief like an onion, burning
the eyes to tears, the nose to unseemly red,
disturbs the stately ceremony of mourning
which should have all the reserve of the mourned dead,

and ought to be smooth as the motors of Cadillacs,
and lucid as headlights burning in the daylight.
Grief, like ammonia spirits in little packs,
should be, if on hand, somewhere out of sight.

It all went properly. The prayers were spoken
in a fine voice, and with most professional frown,
but even machines go wrong, and the heart was broken
by the keening pulleys that lowered her casket down.

CESSNA 170

A mechanical thing,
a left wheel brake:
but it grabbed and the light plane spun
left, and the right wing,
like a chicken bone, almost inaudibly broke;
and the right wheel had collapsed
and the door was gone.

The wind blew
still in the windsock
where, at the far end of the field,
we watched the emergency crew
come clanging out in the toy-red fire truck
racing against the gas
the cowl had spilled

and that gleamed beneath
a steady sun on the metal.
O, I have read those tales of heroes
gone down to dusty death
in a moment of honor, recklessly, and in battle,
and martyrs, beautiful victims
of crazy Neroes,

but for premiums paid
and my double indemnity clause
I gave thanks quickly, working
at the ingeniously made
safety belt catch, and for liability laws,
while I wriggled under the wing
and when I was walking.

No one was hurt.
They covered the nose with foam,
and later, the ungainly tow-truck appeared
and left a dent in the dirt,
the service entrance of Proserpine's dark home,
known no better now,
and no less feared.

TREE WORSHIP

Below this apparent tree, the mirrored other
branches into the dark as this into light;
the bottom is not bottom, then, but middle,
and earth no earth, but the bisecting plane,
a surface, as the exemplary tree's subsurface,
outside the wood, inside the bark, carries
the sap up, but torn through, all around,
brings the whole tree down.
                              Hearts are pulp
and the core of the earth is probably molten nickel.
You, who are fascinated by your dark organs
where sword thrust or gunshot will bring blood
and let life dribble out, must study trees:
the hollow trees are thoroughfares for spirits
where those of the earth come up to meet those of the air;
and live trees, keeping with root and branch
the earth and air together, make that surface,
the precarious film, the leaf-thin skin we walk on,
holding through ring after dangerous tree ring.

THEODORIC

To Ravenna, Livonian amber, the rich pelts
of Swedish sables, and horses, one after another—
white horses with their jewelled saddles and bridles—
or ornamental armor. In return
Theodoric sent sundials, water clocks;
in exchange for slaves, musicians, to proclaim
the enlightenment of his Italy, its culture.
To keep the Romans from ruining their buildings,
he forbade the taking of marble from monuments,
prohibited carving initials, and proscribed
drawing obscene pictures on the arches.

For thirty-two years he ruled, but by the end
he had ceased to care, and with Boethius
he dealt in the obvious way: for conspiracy,
death. And the grief of Symmachus *was* excessive,
indiscrete, and, finally, seditious.
Him too Theodoric killed, having learned at last
that when in Rome ...
                    At dinner the next week,
a giant turbot from the Adriatic
turned in Theodoric's eyes to the fury
of the dead Symmachus, the open angry eye,
the sharp teeth, the rows of shining teeth.
The emperor went to bed and lay three days
trembling with cold beneath the bedclothes,
loose in the bowels and mumbling to his doctor
of repentance and disgust, and died mumbling.

And afterwards, his daughter built him a chapel
in Ravenna, his favorite city, and his remains
she placed there in a vase of porphyry—
the remains of the emperor and of his dream
of the city that once had been, that ought to be.
They threw it into the crater of Lipari,
to consign him finally into the infernum
and teach him the Roman secret of letting go.

FIRST SNOW
For Sarah

The white is arbitrary. It could have been blue,
falling in blue flakes from the blue sky,
or pink, the color of cold of the bathroom tiles.
But the evenness is impressive, the planes, the too
graded, too smooth yard, street tidied by
this wet, white whim that stretches on for miles.

Footprints, however. She experiments with a boot,
then willful looping about the lawn. She is
all seriousness as, in her red snowsuit,
she stamps along in her anabasis
to civilize this wilderness. Her tracks
make random roads, approximate a town.
She laughs. She sits in the snow. She can relax
and play in it, now that nature has been put down.

BELISARIUS

At last Belisarius, cleared of the charge of treason,
regained his titles, had his wealth returned,
and eight months later died, honorably.
And if Justinian confiscated then
most of the estate, it was no insult.
The emperor often confiscated estates,
and the widow was left with something, and of course,
the affair had been embarassing, after all.

That "Give a penny to Belisarius"
is only a fiction of John Tzetzes, monk
and sentimentalist. The general
was not blinded, never had to beg,
never said any such thing.
                        But the tale endures
because it is horrible and not surprising,
and, having saved the city from the Bulgars,
having been great, he ought to have come to begging.

One does develop a taste for this grinding down.

SPECULATIONS ABOUT THE DEATH OF ESKIMOS

I have often imagined the moment—on the white
moonlit ice in the black of polar water,
its erratic pitch and yaw, the wind's bite
and the shapes on shore of son, grandson, granddaughter

still as whalebone, gazing as I go.
I once tried to build an igloo, thought the dogsled
fun—I liked dogs—but the Eskimo,
with his fur-fringed, weather-worn face, filled me with dread,

shipping his relatives off on the ice to die—
to freeze? to starve? to drown? I couldn't decide,
for I was always on that ice floe by
some terrible mistake. On shore, they cried

and were sorry to learn, too late, how much they loved me.
It is not like that at all, but very formal,
undemonstrative, done with some dignity.
Death is not melodramatic but, properly, normal.

And the cause of death is almost certainly freezing,
which is painless, quick, cleaner than razor or pill,
rifle, rope, or guillotine for easing
the last agonies. So gently does cold kill

and so familiar is it to Eskimos
that tears are unlikely indeed. The departure itself
is visibly simple. The strip of water grows
wider and wider between floe and ice shelf;

neither physician nor priest is required to say
which moment is the last; it is perfectly clear
that there he is, slowly drifting away.
Calmly they wait for him to disappear.

And out of sight of the shore, the sting of the cold,
and the sting abating. The feet begin to feel numb.
It happens so slowly; slowly one grows old,
one learns the patience to wait for death to come.

The flab around the middle, the slack skin,
the defeats that flesh has suffered are undone:
the wattles wed again to the firm chin,
the fat is hard as bone, the bone as stone.

That I have changed my mind in twenty years
is reasonable. My fear was a child's fault.
I make my way and that cold shore appears
not unattractive as I start to smell salt.

HALF FARE: A suite for Evan

London

You mustn't miss the criminals
in Mme. Tussaud's waxworks.
You can see their horrible weapons,
you can see their awful smirks.
The waxworks figures there
have a tendency to stare
but it's nothing to scare you—relax,
for they're none of them real, but wax.
But when I asked a guard
how to get to Scotland Yard,
and he stood as still as a wall
and as quiet, I thought he was hard
of hearing and that was all.
But the guard was a waxwork, too,
which was terrible of them to do.
Much worse than the criminal crew,
which seemed then to be standing still, you
know, waiting around to kill you,
the minute those guards of wax
had turned their protective backs.

Barcelona

I'd like to own a
little villa
several kilo-
meters out
of Barcelona.
There's no doubt
but that I'd have a
terrific time
on the Costa Brava.
How sublime

to tell a friend,
"Come as you are,
but with *maillot de bain*
and perhaps a guitar."

Rome

Rome is fountains,
Rome is stairs,
Rome is cardinals, saying prayers—
for Rome is churches
and Rome is masses,
but Rome is everyone in sunglasses,
riding around in little cars,
and looking just like movie stars.
Rome is the home of the Coliseum.
Rome is museum after museum.
But what I think about Rome is nice is
the wonderful man with Italian ices.

Florence

You know it's really very phony
on the Via Tornabuoni
where Americans in much too sporty dress
assume their very casual stances
and ignore each other's glances
or exclaim, "How odd to see you," at American Express.

So let us go from this farrago
(fancy Florence as Chicago!),
cross the Arno and walk five blocks to the west,
where behind Palazzo Pitti
there is really the most pretty
spot, The Boboli. "The Boboli?" (How could you not have guessed?)

Up the avenues of hedges
or along the landscaped edges
of the vistas, one could wander for a week.
There is beauty in God's plenty,
but the youthful cognoscenti
come to Boboli, to Boboli, to play at hide and seek.

St. Tropez

The proper way
in St. Tropez
is not
to go into a restaurant,
but have them bring the meal you want
to the yacht.

And the proper sport
along the port
is greeting
with a friendly eye
the passers-by
who are looking at what you're eating.

Vezelay

Hooray, hooray
for the monks who play
the phonograph
at Vezelay.
Masses, magnificats, requiems,
at so and so many RPMs.

It may seem a little secular,
but with the Romanesque,
what misses the spectacular
at least is picturesque.

Paris

Daddy did not want to bruise
our feelings at the Deux Magots,
and let us order something, so
we chose a limonade gazeuse.
    Oh, how exceedingly soigné
    of Seven-up to sound that way!

The Channel

How odd to be on a train
from England across to France,
for on the train you remain
while also you go on a boat.
A curious circumstance!
The passengers do not change
from train to boat—they arrange
to pull up the boat to the quay
and get the train on that way,
and still in the train you float
across the channel. And I
have wondered ever since, why
you couldn't transship your car
on the train on the boat. There are
so many wonderful ways
of getting around these days:
on skates on a bike in a car
on a train on a boat—how far
you could get in a couple of months,
with everything going at once!

Vienna

Austria! For Austria
    I'm really quite insane.
To have gone, and not to have been in Wien
    Would have been to have gone in vain.

Paris

On the second Thursday and fourth are tours,
they tell me, of the Parisian sewers.
You meet at the statue of Lille in the Place
de la Concorde, and from there, en masse,
you go in sewers in boats, with a guide,
and it sounds like a perfectly wonderful ride.

Or anyway, that is what I've heard,
    But Mother always arranges it so,
        that no matter how much I'd like to go,
we seem to hit Paris first Thursdays and third.

Venice

The friendly gondolier named Guido
maneuvers in the canals of Venice,
poling along, avoiding the menace
of the motorized monster, the vaporetto.

For anyplace you want to get, "Ho,
gondola!" is what you shout,
and the friendly gondolier named Guido
will bring his gondola about

and take you across to visit the Lido.
If you ask him to take you back, "Si,"
he will say, and his water taxi
will wait for you. He will ask you, "Dove?"

    (Italian for *Where?*)
                And for something of a
treat, you tell him, "San Marco Square."

There is a church, and, of course, religion's
fine, but look for the thousands of pigeons
flying and strutting about. It's grand
and if you hold still, they will eat from your hand.

Vevey

In Switzerland, you have to save a
day to stay and play in Vevey.
Near the shore of the lake, where the water is shallow,
you can go for a ride in a little pedallo,
which is a boat you can peddle on,
painted and shaped to look like a swan.
The sky is blue
                and the water too,
and the mountains with snow complete the view

which is all there is to this little spot,
excepting the excellent chocolat.

Avignon

When the lights go on
in Avignon
all over the palace wall,
it's a wonderful sight,
a jewel in the night—
but so is the city hall
which is right next door,
as a matter of fact,
the lovely electric display
gives an undeniable beauty to
the Crédit Lyonais,
which is a bank between the two.
And if a garage were there,
the gasoline pumps would look marvelous
rising up in a brilliant glare.
When I get home, I intend to buy
electric bulbs by the case,
and illuminate our house at night
with spotlights all over the place.
And people will come from miles around
and stare with their eyes so wide,
and say what a gorgeous house it is,
and wonder who lives inside.

Copenhagen

      You can get to Copenhagen
      overnight inside a Wagon-
         Lit
      Which is a Pullman car gone frivolous,
      the Parc Monceau a trifle Tivolous,
         a Danish pastry that has turned *pâtisserie*.

ELEGY FOR WALTER STONE

In August of 1959, I interviewed John Hall Wheelock at his home in Easthampton, N.Y., on the occasion of the publication of Poets of Today VI, *which Mr. Wheelock edited and which included the poetry of Messrs. Gene Baro, Donald Finkel, and Walter Stone.*

I

In the Apache over Hempstead with Finkel's view
of Fuji and the great wave in my hand...
But who would pretend to care? And why should Finkel
(not this particular Finkel, but any Finkel)
have a view of Fuji?
                        So I wondered whether
there was a first-rate delicatessen in all Japan.
An odd business this—when the mind takes off
leaving the body's ground, and the old terrain
with height is suddenly strange and unfamiliar,
when woods are smoothed to shrubbery, to lawn,
to plain green as the U.S. on a map,
when a Fuji is smoothed to paint, and paint to print,
and a craggy Finkel to an anonymous voice.
And the last is worst.
                        In London, on a grant
to study Renaissance eschatology,
the late professor and poet, Walter Stone,
committed suicide: an actual man
ground to a sheaf of poems that follow Finkel's
and in their total commitment to aesthetics
go his one better, for somewhere, still, in hiding,
in Queens, or perhaps the Bronx, surreptitious, Finkel
munches pastrami on rye (and afterwards
his tongue hunts for the caraway seeds in the teeth),
giving less of a damn for Fuji than, even, I.
Vive le Finkel! Which is exactly the point.

But let me be honest, for I too am a poet,
and the poet, Stone, is survived by a poet, his wife,

Ruth. And by Finkel (not my conceit, but the real
Donald Finkel, who lives and teaches at Bard),
and by his former students,
                              and by three daughters
who ought to despise that rising, the lyric thrust
that can take a man up where he only guesses at Hempstead,
sees something important in a dead Japanese volcano,
writes—as Stone did—stanzas about a spider
so fine he forgets about his daughters and wife,
forgets even himself, and the piece of work
that a man is, speechless and on the earth.

II

Later: at night: remembering the plane
and the quick trip out to visit John Hall Wheelock.
We savored the horror of it on the porch
and then went in to lunch.
                              Hart Crane
I can understand. Jumping overboard
was, for him, the perfectly fitting gesture,
with all the grief of his failings as a man,
and still a passing insult to his readers
who cared for the wrong and expendable things.
                                          But Stone
envied the angels' monotonous excellence,
their tuning-fork perfection, their effortlessness,
and even perhaps their wings...
                              The weights of the world
he shrugged off him, as if in a moment of pique:
his shoes, for example, in rows on some closet floor;
and his family, and his automobile, and his hairbrush;
and Vassar College itself where the grass grows green
and the laundry washes two thousand bras a week.
The stupid stuff of the world...
                              He renounced it all,
or perhaps it was a kind of an embrace,
to become, after an unpleasant moment of choking
(or do you feel even that? Does the neck snap
like a pretzel stick and the life go out in an instant

without that terrible dwindling?), like a stone,
like a table, a part of that same dumb stuff
(with a frozen smile for the possible play on his name).
Not merely the notion of rest, but to be a part
of the created world, to rot, to change,
to become absolutely chemical, and Godly:
this, perhaps, is more the poet's delusion,
fitting the paradoxical turn of the mind
which rejects itself by its own final thought.
Suddenly, there he was, as dead as a door,
and full of the same dignity as the door
in its wonderful knowledge of the real nature of substance.

Or did he wander off in that dark wood
to visit the *malebolges*, where they talk
in terza rima, suddenly convinced...
But no!
        Next I'll be calling out the dolphins
and making him into a hapless youth.
                                            He died
taking his motive with him, and leaving us
to guess what his question was that had no answer,
and to think, with awe, of a man dead in his prime.

III

The plane banked to the left and suddenly landed
as gracefully as a sea bird on a rock,
and I stepped out into the forenoon sun
and the salt smell of the wind coming off the ocean,
and felt that slight irrational sense of relief
that the plane had made it all right, and I was standing
there, on the ground, waving to Mr. Wheelock
who had a cab there, waiting. He told me how
he had once refused to go up in a plane with Lindbergh,
and smiled and remarked on the weather as we rode.
Nineteenth century outside and eighteenth in,
his house stands on a rise with a grove of trees
around it. Seventy summers it has been
standing there, where no other house is in view,

and seventy summers John Hall Wheelock has lived
through the rooms of his father's house, and over the lawns.
But it is not virtue:
                     some of the good die young,
and some live long, and life is a random thing,
and the bus careens indifferently up on the sidewalk,
and the lightning, witless, streaks down into the park,
and the virus floats on the universal air.
It is not virtue, but a lucky chance
to which we attach perhaps too much importance
(and how we despise any quitting while you're ahead).
Wheelock was calm about it—regretful, but calm—
as we talked of Walter Stone, and then moved on
to talk of poetry or old pewter,
but there is no changing of subject at seventy-three,
and all the time he talked in one gentle tone
of the various guises of the one same thing
that a man must learn to gaze at, more and more:
Stone dead, and the poems left behind,
and the poems he would leave himself, and the pewter
and the house his father left, and the afternoon
perceptibly giving way.
                     Never mind how,
and never mind even when. All death is nature's,
whether by germ in the blood or idea in the head,
or sudden mischance in the wasteful order of things.
Gaze fixedly at it, and the distinctions
disappear.
          An unintellectual sadness
and a dumb calm is all I can summon up
for Walter Stone, for Wheelock, for myself,
for the act of imagination in Finkel's Fuji—
for all these sparks struck off by the turning world.

www.ingramcontent.com/pod-product-compliance
Lightning Source LLC
Chambersburg PA
CBHW031715230426
43668CB00006B/218